DIVAN of RUDAKI

DIVAN of RUDAKI

Translations and Introduction

Paul Smith

NEW HUMANITY BOOKS

Book Heaven
Booksellers & Publishers

NEW HUMANITY BOOKS

BOOK HEAVEN

(Booksellers & Publishers for over 40 years)

47 Main Road Campbells Creek

Victoria 3451 Australia

www.newhumanitybooks.com

ISBN: 978-1722991609

Persian Poetry/Sufism/Sufi Poetry/Iranian Poetry

CONTENTS

Bust of Rudaki (Wikipedia)

Persian Poetry: A New Beginning

The Muslim Conquest meant to Persia in many respects what the Norman Conquest meant to England. The battles of Kadisia and Nahavand (637, 642 A.D.) were the Hastings of Persia; and with the killing of the last Sasanian king in 651, Persia came under the Muslim rule of the Arabs. There followed in consequence, an infiltration of foreign blood and a certain amount of fusion in language and a partial blending in thought. But beyond the sacrifice, great as it was of giving up the old national religion of Zoroastrianism, vanquished Iran yielded little more to the victorious Arab than Britain gave up to the invading Norman.

If the Persian vocabulary took on something of a foreign tinge the poetry flowed the smoother because of it; and if the freedom of religious thought was fettered for a time by the bonds of Islam... the true Persian spirit threw off the shackles two centuries later, when it achieved a semi-independence of its own on the decline of the Caliphate at Baghdad in the ninth century and with this emancipation began the re-establishment of its national life and laid the foundations for a renaissance in the realm of poetry.

Beginnings may be small but great results may follow. Such was the case with the re-born art of poetry in Persia. Poetry, nursed for two hundred years by the fostering care of three princely dynasties of Iranian blood, Tahirid (820-872), Saffarid (860-903) and Samanid (874-999), not to mention the Buwaihids (also of the tenth century), or the eleventh century Ghaznavids of Afghanistan, was destined to grow in grace and stature until the thin register of its voice changed into the strong tone of a Firdausi with all the virility of the race within its compass.

The mastery of the newer speech with its infusion of Arabic (the Pahlavi tongue having now been transformed into New Persian) was already complete, and could develop only in range and power of expression. The language, in fact, has ever since remained essentially the same, so that Persian has changed far less in a thousand years than has English in the comparatively brief period from Shakespeare to the present.

The cradle of the literary renaissance was Eastern Iran or the provinces of Khurasan and Transoxiana. The city of Merv, the ruins of which may still be visited in the environs of the modern town that perpetuates the name in Turkistan, was the scene. This ancient city, the Zoroastrian 'Marghu' of the Avesta, and 'Queen of the World,' as it was called in medieval times had witnessed the death of the last Sasanian king, but was destined to witness also the rebirth of Persian poetry, for within its walls was born Abbas of Merv to whom tradition, rightly or wrongly, ascribes as being the earliest minstrel to chant poetry in the new Persian tongue... and Rudaki was the first great Master of it.

Source: Early Persian Poetry... From the Beginnings Down to the Time of Firdausi by A.V. Williams Jackson The Macmillan Company New York 1920. (Pages 14-16).

Rudaki depicted as blind poet on Iranian stamp. (Wikipedia)

The Life, Times & Poetry of Rudaki

Abu 'Abd Allah Ja'far ibn Muhammad Rudaki (858-941) the 'father of Persian Poetry' and possibly the *ruba'i*, was born in the village of Rudak (hence his pen-name or *takhallus*) in Transoxania near Samarkand. The historian and biographer 'Awfi says that Rudaki was blind from birth, but other historians of the time disagree with him asking how one could create such images of nature if he did not at one time see. Others say that a ruler later in his life held red-hot iron rods before his eyes and blinded him when he refused to compose poetry for him. This is now generally accepted.

First a wandering 'dervish' poet/minstrel he later served at the court of the Samanids of Bokhara. Rudaki was so intelligent and like Hafiz of Shiraz (1320-1392) blessed with such a fine memory that by the age of eight he had memorized all of the *Koran*.

He is said to have had a happy childhood spending much of his time listening to stories and songs and learning about his people's ways and aspirations. He began to compose poems expressing their desires and his own. He had a beautiful voice and was a fine musician, playing the harp, and because of this he mixed freely with other minstrels and with musicians and dancers.

His harp teacher was the famous Bakhtiar and he eventually excelled his master. He traveled the Tajikistan highlands with his master, singing and creating songs. When Bakhtiar died and left him his famous harp he continued wandering and singing until his fame reached Bokhara.

Nasr ibn Ahmad summoned him to his court and he prospered there amassing great wealth. He had 200 slaves in his retinue... and 400 camels carried his belongings when he traveled.

Nizami Arudi of Samarkand writing in his 'Chahar Maqala' or 'Four Discourses' probably in 1011, only 60 years after Rudaki's death, states (as translated by E.G. Browne in 1921... see Selected Bibliography)... "Now the poet must be of tender temperament, profound in thought, sound in genius, clear of vision, quick of insight. He must be well versed in many divers sciences, and quick to extract what is best from his environment; for as poetry is of advantage in every science, so is every science of advantage in poetry. And the poet must be of pleasing conversation in social gatherings, of cheerful countenance on festive occasions; and his verse must have attained to such a level that it is written on the page of Time and celebrated on the lips and tongues of the noble, and be such that they transcribe it in books and recite it in cities. For the richest portion and most excellent part of poetry is immortal fame, and until it be thus confirmed and published it is ineffectual to this end, and this result cannot accrue from it; it will not survive its author, and, being ineffectual for the immortalizing of his name, how can it confer immortality on another?

But to this rank a poet cannot attain unless in the prime of his life and the season of his youth he commits to memory 20,000 couplets of the poetry of the Ancients, holds them constantly before his eyes, and continually reads and marks the *divans* of the masters of his art, observing how they have acquitted themselves in the strait passes and delicate places of song, in order that thus the fashion and varieties of verse may become ingrained in his nature, and the defects and beauties of poetry may be inscribed on the tablet of his understanding. In this way his style will improve and his genius will develop. Then, when his taste has been formed by wide reading of poetry, and his style of expression is thus strengthened, let him address himself seriously to the poetic art, study the science of Prosody, and peruse the works of master Abu'l-Hasan Baharami of

Sarakhs, such as the 'Goal of Prosodists' (*Ghayatu'l-'Arudiyyin*), the 'Thesaurus of Rhyme' (*Kanzu'l-Qafiya*), and the works treating poetic ideas and phraseology, plagiarisms, biographies, and all the sciences of this class, with such a master as he deems best, that thus he in turn may come to merit the title of Master, that his name may remain on the page of time like the names of those other masters which we have mentioned, and that he may be able to able to discharge his debt to his patron and lord for what he obtains from him, so that his name may endure for ever.

Now it behooves the King to patronize such a person, so that he may remain in his service and celebrate his praise. But if he fall below this level, he should waste no money on him and pay no heed to his poetry, especially if he be old:; for I have investigated this matter, and in the whole world have found nothing worse than an old poet, nor any money more ill spent than what is given to such. For one so ignoble as not to have discovered in fifty years that what he writes is bad, when will he discover it? But if he be young and has the right talent, even though his verse be not good, there is some hope that it may improve, and according to the Law of Chivalry it is proper to patronize him, a duty to take care of him, and an obligation to maintain him.

Now in the service of kings naught is better than improvisation, for thereby the king's mood is cheered, his receptions are made brilliant, and the poet himself attains his object. Such favours as Rudaki obtained from the House of Saman by his improvisations and by virtue of his verse, none other hath experienced.

They relate thus, that Nasr bin Ahmad, who was the central point of the Samanid group, whose fortunes reached their zenith during the days of his rule, was most plenteously equipped with every means of enjoyment and material of splendour – well filled treasuries, an efficient army, and loyal servants. In winter he used to reside at Bokhara, the capital, while in summer he used to reside at Samarqand or some other of the cities of Khurasan. Now one year it was the turn of Herat. He spent the spring at Badghis, where are the most charming pasture-grounds of Khurasan and Iraq, for there are nearly a thousand watercourses abounding in water and pasture, any one of which would suffice for an army.

When the beasts had well eaten, and had regained their strength and condition, and were fit for warfare or to take the field, Nasr bin Ahmad turned his face toward Herat but halted outside the city of Marghazar-i-Sapid and there pitched his camp. Cool breezes from the north were stirring, and the fruit was ripening in the districts of Malin and Karukh – fruit which can be obtained in but few places, and nowhere so cheaply. There the army rested. The climate was charming, the breeze cool, food plentiful, fruit abundant, and the air filled with fragrant scents, so that the soldiers enjoyed their life to the full during the spring and summer. When Mihregan (autumn festival) arrived, and the juice of the grape came into season, and the eglantine, basil and yellow rocket were in bloom, they did full justice to the charms of autumn, and took their fill of the pleasures of that season. Mihregan was protracted, for the cold did not wax severe, and the grapes proved to be of exceptional sweetness. For in the district of Herat one hundred and twenty different varieties of the grape occur, each sweeter and more delicious than the other; and amongst them are in particular two kinds which are not to be found in any other region of the inhabited world, one called *Tarniyan* and the other *Gulchidi,* tight-skinned, and luscious, so that you would surely say they were (flavoured with) cinnamon. A cluster of Gulchidi grapes sometimes attains a weight of five maunds; they are black with pitch and sweet as sugar, nor can one eat many for the sweetness that is in them. And besides these there were all sorts of other delicious fruits.

So the Amir Nasr bin Ahmad saw Mihregan and its fruits, and was mightily pleased therewith. Then the narcissus began to bloom, and the raisins were plucked and stoned in Malin, and hung up on lines, and packed in chests; and the Amir with his army moved into the two groups of hamlets called Ghura and Darwaz. There he saw mansions of which one was like the highest paradise, having before it a garden or pleasure-ground with a northern aspect. There they wintered, while the Mandarin oranges began to arrive from Sistan and the sweet oranges from Mazandaran; and so they passed the winter in the most agreeable manner.

When (the second) spring came, the Amir sent the horses to Badghis and moved his camp to Malin (to a spot) between two streams. And when summer came, the fruits again ripened; and when Mihregan came, he said, 'Let us enjoy Mihregan at Herat'; and so from season to season he continued to procrastinate, until four years had passed in this way. For it was then the heyday of the Samanian prosperity, and the land was flourishing, the kingdom unmenaced by foes, the army loyal, fortune favourable, and heaven auspicious; yet withal the Amir's attendants grew weary, and desire for home arose within them, while they beheld the King quiescent, the air of Herat in his heart; and in the course of conversation he would declare that he preferred Herat to the Garden of Eden, and would set its charms above those of the springtime of Beauty.

So they perceived that he intended to remain there for that summer also. Then the captains of the army and courtiers of the King went to Abu 'Abdullah Rudaki, than whom there were none more honoured of the King's intimates, and none whose words found so ready an acceptance. And they said to him: 'We will present thee with five thousand *dinars* if thou wilt contrive some artifice whereby the King may be induced to depart hence, for our hearts are dying for desire of our wives and children, and our souls are like to leave us for longing after Bokhara.' Rudaki agreed; and since he had felt the Amir's pulse and understood his temper, he perceived that prose would not affect him, and so had recourse to verse. He therefore composed a *qasida;* and, when the Amir had taken his morning cup, came in and did obeisance, and sat down in his place; and, when the musicians ceased, he took up his harp, and, playing 'Lover's Air,' began this elegy:--

Fragrance of stream Muliyan to me keeps coming:

friends left behind into my memory, keeps coming.

Then he strikes a lower key and sings:--

Sands of the Oxus bank, although they are rough,

beneath our feet as soft and silky... keeps coming.

See greeting of the Jihan, joyful at friends return...

rising waist-high to embrace fondly, keeps coming.

O Bokhara, live for a long time and be happy... for

joyfully your prince, your life to see, keeps coming.

Bokhara, you are the moon and your prince the sky:

into the sky's vault, moon obviously keeps coming.

Bokhara is the garden and the prince is a cypress…

cypress to the garden to grow freely keeps coming.

When Rudaki reached this verse, the Amir was so much affected that he descended from his throne, bestrode the horse which was on sentry duty, and set off for Bokhara so precipitately that they carried his riding-boots after him for two *parasangs*, as far as Buruna, and only then did he put them on; nor did he draw rein anywhere till he reached Bokhara, and Rudaki received from the army the double of that five thousand *dinars*.

In Samarqand, in the year A.H. 504 (= A.D. 1110-1111), I heard from the Dihqan Abu Rija Ahmad b. 'Abdu's-Samad al-'Abidi as follows:-- 'My grandfather, the Dihqan Abu Rija, related that (on this occasion) when Rudaki reached Samarqand, he had four hundred camels laden with his wealth.' And, indeed, that illustrious man was worthy of this splendid equipment, for no one has yet produced an imitation of that elegy, nor found means to surmount triumphantly the difficulties 9which the subject presents). Thus the poet-laureate Mu'izzi was one of the sweetest singers and most graceful wits in Persia, and his poetry reaches the highest level in freshness and sweetness, and excels in fluency and charm. Zaynu'l-Mulk Abu Sa'd (b.) Hindu b. Muhammad b. Hindu of Isfahan requested him to compose an imitation of this *qasida,* and Mu'izzi, unable to plead his inability so to so, wrote:--

Rustom now from Mazandaran keeps coming,

now Zayn-i-Mulk from Isfahan keeps coming.

All wise men will perceive how great is the difference between this poetry and that; for who can sing with such sweetness as does Rudaki when he says:--

Renown and praise are a lasting gain, surely;

even though royal coffers loss sustain, surely!

For in this couplet are seven admirable touches of art: first, the verse is apposite; secondly, antithetical; thirdly, it has a refrain; fourthly, it embodies an enunciation of equivalence; fiftly, it has sweetness; sixthly, style; seventhly, energy. Every master of the craft, who has deeply considered the poetic art, will admit, after a little reflection, that I am right." (End of quote. All trans. of poetry by Paul Smith)

He was commissioned and paid 40,000 *dirhams* to translate *Kalila and Dimna* (a collection of fables originating in India and translated into Arabic in 750) into Persian verse (*masnavi*... rhyming couplets). This work, plus most of the reported massive 1,300,000 couplets, some say 130,000, that he composed (his *Divan*) have not survived the ravages of time. There remain only about 75 poems... *qasidas, ghazals* and *ruba'is and qit'as* (most here translated). Of his epic masterpieces we have nothing beyond a few lines.

Rudaki is said to have invented the metre that the *ruba'i* is usually composed in. One New Year's Festival *(Nowruz)* he happened to be strolling in a garden where some children played with nuts and one threw a walnut along a groove in a stick and it jumped out then rolled back again creating a sound and the children shouted with delight in imitation, *'Ghaltan ghaltan hami ravad ta bun-i gau,' (Ball, ball, surprising hills to end of a brave try)*. Rudaki immediately recognized in the line's metre a new invention and by the repetition four times of the *rhyme* he had quickly created a *ruba'i*... and is considered the first master of this form.

The poetess Rabi'a who was also known as 'The daughter of Ka'b' was said by Farid al-din 'Attar to have become royalty, her father first becoming king and then her brother. She is the first female poet who composed in Persian whose name and some poems have come down to us. Born in Balkh (now

Afghanistan) in the 10th century there are many legends about her unhappy love affair.

After her father died he put her in charge of her brother Harith. Her love affair with a slave named Bektash where they sent each other love letters in verse was said to have inspired Rida-Quli-Khan Hidayat (d.1871) to compose the romantic epic *Bektash-Nama* influenced by Farid al-din 'Attar where in his masterpiece *Ilahi-nama* ('Book of God') he tells the story of their tragic love affair and her meeting with Rudaki.

Rudaki was so amazed by her wonderful poetry and upset by her tragic love-story that she had confided in him… that he, in a drunken state a short time later revealed the secret of her love for handsome Bektash by quoting her poems when drunk which inadvertently caused her death when they were overheard by her jealous brother. 'Attar quotes one of her marvelous poem-messages to Bektash and her passionate, gut-wrenching *masnavi* written in her own blood on the prison walls where she was locked in by bricks and mortar by her brother until she died, for loving this slave. (For her life and poems see my 'Princesses, Sufis, Dervishes & Martyrs: Ten Great Women Poets of the East' New Humanity Books 2014.)

In 937 he fell out of favour at court (perhaps he was blinded at this time as some commentators suggest) after the death of the prime-minister who had supported him. His life ended in abject poverty, forgotten by the world at that time (see first *qasida* below), perhaps the reason why so much of his vast output has not survived. Rudaki died in Rudak in 941.

Rudaki's poetry is about the passage of time, old age, death, fortune's fickleness, importance of the matters of the heart, the need to be happy. Although he praised kings, nobles and heroes... his greatest love was knowledge and experience.

He is considered the first 'great' poet of the classical Persian language and the 'father of Persian poetry' although a few other poets composed in the new language before him such as Abbas of Merv (d. 815-16) who 'Awfi in his *Lubab al-albab,* one of the oldest treatises on the history of Persian poetry (13th century), an anthology and biography of the first poets, attributes the first poem in the new language of Persian... that later became known as 'Classical Persian'. Recent studies on this subject (see Rypka below) have also come to the conclusion that this is correct.

The occasion that inspired the *qit'a* was said to be the triumphant return of the Caliph Mamun, the son of Harun ar-Rashid of 'Arabian Nights' fame. Abbas, being a poet, was chosen to compose a poem in praise of this event and even though he usually composed in Arabic, he decided to use his native Persian to mark the event. Only the first two couplets have come down to us through 'Awfi's book.

Before me, no poet has poem this way ever sung;

in the Persian tongue there is of poetry, nothing:

this is why I choose this language to praise you,

so your majesty, grace, charm it will be winning.

It seems that Hanzalah (mid. 9th C.) of Baghis (a district north-west of Herat) was inspired by Abbas of Merv's example and began to compose poems in Persian. 'Awfi says of his poetry, 'the graceful flow of his expression is like the water of Paradise and his couplets are fresh like cool wine and likeable like the north wind'. His poems became so popular that his were probably the first to be collected into a *Divan,* but unfortunately like many of these early poets, only a few fragments remain. In what some scholars say is the first *ruba'i* (but of a different metre than that discovered by Rudaki and in which most *ruba'is* were composed after that, with the exception of those of Baba Tahir)... Hanzalah warns his sweetheart that it is futile to throw rue-seed on fire to avoid the influence of the evil eye, an old superstition.

Though my sweetheart rue-seed on fire threw

so that from the evil eye no hurt would accrue:

what is the use of fire and rue-seed to that one

whose face is like fire... mole, like seed of rue?

On hearing the following *qit'a* by him the ass-herder Ahmad of Khujistan was so moved into action that he eventually became the Amir of Khurasan!

If lordship in the lion's mouth lies, be brave,

grab it from lion's mouth... snatch it away!

Go for pomp, honour, wealth, rank... or like

hero look death in face and come what may.

Firuz (died approx 890). Firuz al-Machriki (the Easterner). 'Awfi called his poems 'sweeter than a stolen kiss'. Two *qita's* of his...

Bird is an arrow, "Strange," one might say...

a bird that makes its prey some living thing.

Arrow receives from eagle gift of its plume,

then to its doom its own brood, it does bring!

O those beautiful teeth, lips exquisitely formed,

they make me burn forever with love's passion!

Teeth flashing as bright as the Pleiades above,

lips like halo of moonlight round the full moon!

There was also Abu Salik who died at the end of the 9th century. 'Awfi says Abu Salik of Gurgan 'spread out the carpet of words and raised aloft the banner of eloquence'. A *qit'a* of his...

If you can shed your own blood on this earth,

for it's better to shed your own pure honour:

far better to worship an idol than some man;

listen, remember and practice this, you hear?

Abu Shakur of Balkh (d. mid 10th century) appeared before both Shahid and Rudaki and is said to have from both of them 'carried off the ball of excellence'. He was a bi-lingual poet and the earliest poet to use the *mutakarib* metre in his epic *masnavi Afarin-Nama* composed in 948 that Firdausi used much later in his Shah-Nama. He composed two other *masnavis* in different metres.

He claimed he couldn't speak a lie to his beloved, because that 'would tie his neck into a yoke'. His style is simple, some of his poems are like jingles, or child-like. Perhaps he was the originator of the *ruba'i* (see below) or perhaps he too like Shahid (to follow) got the *ruba'i* metre off Rudaki... they all being alive at the same time. His *ruba'i*...

From stabs of grief for you, I am laid low;

bowed down by separation's burden, I go.

I washed hands of your wiles and tricks...

none had moods, whims like yours I know.

Qit'a...

There was a pauper, so father did say,

who sank so low he begged for bread:

door to door dry bread he begged for...

his trade, until that day, he was dead.

Like Abbas of Merv and Shahid (to follow) Abdullah Muhammad al-Junaidi (10th century) was skilled in composing both prose and poetry. His drinking song (below) is perhaps the earliest.

At dawn take a long drink from the flagon of wine,

as cock crows and lute makes its sorrowful whine.

When the sun raises its head over the crest of hill,

it began to blush from cup filled with grape of vine.

From the cup to the couch when the night comes...

from the couch to the cup... as day begins to shine.

Just like milk is the food that for an infant is best,

let old men their diet... to milk of the grape confine!

Shahid of Balkh (d. 937) was mourned in a poem by his friend Rudaki (see below). He was said to be 'of excellent mind, a spirited conversationalist, with high opinions and a scholar'. The melancholy that is in some of his poems meant that he was eventually called, 'the pessimist of the century'. He was said to be one of the great philosophers of his time. In the following *ruba'i* probably composed after those of his friend Rudaki he laments over the ruins of Tus in Khurasan that had been devastated by invading hordes.

Last night by the ruins of Tus I passed by,

seeing owl sitting in place of peacock saw I.

I asked, "What do you know of these ruins?"

It answered, "News is, O no... I could cry!"

Qit'a...

If grief had any smoke as has the blazing fire,

the world would be forever in darkness, blind:

if you travel this world... one end to another,

any wise man totally happy you will not find.

The Rudaki music ensemble conducted by Saeid Khavarnejad and accompanied by singer Alireza Qorbani gave concerts at Vahdat Hall in Teheran to commemorate Abu Abdullah Jafar ibn Mohammad Rudaki in 2008.

UNESCO commemorated the 1150th birth anniversary of Rudaki through holding programs with the support of Afghanistan, Iran, and Tajikistan throughout the year of 2008.

In a press conference the managing director of the Rudaki Foundation Asghar Amirnia, and Mohammadreza Kargar the managing director of Vahdat Hall elaborated on the program. Amirnia said that the idea to form the Rudaki ensemble when first proposed to Tehran's Municipality was rejected, but it was later approved by the Rudaki Foundation.

The ensemble features Amid Zebardast on *ney*, Peyman Asheqan and Kuhyar Babaiian on *tar*, Behnam Mo'ayyerian on lute, Armin Khavarnejad on *damam* (percussion with double face), and Hamid Qanbari on *tonbak*.

Rudaki depicted on an Iranian stamp on the commemoration of his 1100th birthday. (Wikipedia)

The Various Forms in the Poetry of Rudaki

The Ruba'i

Many scholars of Persian Poetry believe that the *ruba'i* is the most ancient Persian poetic form that is original to this language and they state that all other classical forms including the *ghazal, qasida, masnavi, qit'a* and others originated in Arabic literature and the metres employed in them were in Arabic poetry in the beginning... this, can be disputed.

The Persian language is a fine intercourse of Arabic (a masculine-sounding language) and Pahlavi (feminine-sounding language) that is mainly a descendant of the profound language of the Spiritual Master Zoroaster... Zend. Sanskrit is also a branch of that ancient language* (e.g. Zend: *garema* or heat is in Sanskrit *gharma,* in Pahlavi is *garma,* Persian... *garm*/ given to us by that prophet whose perfect and profound teachings in the *gathas* of the *Avesta* were composed in a form very close to the *ruba'i* which one might believe could give him the title not only of the founder of the Persian language and people and mysticism... but also of Persian poetry's most individualistic form of poetic expression.

One can trace the origins of this poetical language back almost 7000 years to Zoroaster's time, not merely less than 2600 years... a mistake that most recent scholars made by confusing the last Zoroastian *priest* bearing his name with that of this original Prophet, the *Rasool* or Messiah, who like Moses, led out his people from their original Aryan lands in Bactria, when they were invaded by many hordes of murderous barbarians.

On that remarkable and in many aspects, far-reaching journey, an argument occurred amongst his people when they had reached what we today call India and many left him and settled there and their language eventually evolved into

Sanskrit. Zoroaster then took his remaining followers west and finally settled near Shiraz in Fars, and Zend eventually became Pahlavi and the Aryan language continued west and founded many languages in Europe, including English.

Now as to the origin of the metre of the *ruba'i* I offer two of Zoroaster's poems or *gathas* to enjoy and consider, even though the metre may not be that of the *ruba'i*, the rhyme structure and content are similar.

Wise One, with these short poems I come before You,

praising Your Righteousness, deeds of Good Mind too.

And when I arrive at that bliss that has come to me...

may these poems of this man of insight... come through.

And another...

May good rulers and not evil ones over us be ruling!

O devoted, by doing good works for mankind, bring

rebirth... prepare all this for what's good for all men:

through work in the field, let ox for us be fattening.

The *ruba'i* is a poem of four lines in which usually the first, second and fourth lines rhyme and sometimes with the *radif* (refrain) after the rhyme words... sometimes all four rhyme. It is composed in metres called *ruba'i* metres. Each *ruba'i* is a separate poem in itself and should not be regarded as a part of a long poem as was created by FitzGerald when he translated those he attributed to Omar Khayyam.

The *ruba'i* (as its name implies) is two couplets *(beyts)* in length, or four lines *(misra)*. The *ruba'i* is a different metre from those used in Arabic poetry that preceded it.

How was this metre invented? The accepted story is that Rudaki created this new *metre* of the *hazaj* group which is essential to the *ruba'i*. Shams-e Qais writing two hundred years later about this moment of poetic history and the effect of this new form on the population said the following... "This new poetic form fascinated all classes, rich and poor, ascetic and drunken rebel-outsider *(rend)*, all wanted to participate in it...

the sinful and the good both loved it; those who were so ignorant they couldn't make out the difference between poetry and prose began to dance to it; those with dead hearts who couldn't tell the difference between a donkey braying and reed's wailing and were a thousand miles away from listening to a lute's strumming, offered up their souls for a *ruba'i*. Many young cloistered girls, from passion for the song of a *ruba'i* broke down the doors and their chastity's walls; many matrons from love for a *ruba'i* let loose the braids of their self-restraint."

And so, the *ruba'i* should be eloquent, spontaneous and ingenious. In the *ruba'i* the first three lines serve as an introduction to the fourth that should be sublime, subtle or pithy and clever. As can be seen from the quote by Shams-e Qais above, the *ruba'i* immediately appealed to all levels of society and has done so ever since. The nobility and royalty enjoyed those in praise of them and the commoner enjoyed the short, simple homilies… the ascetic and mystic could think upon epigrams of deep religious fervour and wisdom; the reprobates enjoyed the subtle and amusing satires and obscenities... and for everyone, especially the cloistered girls and old maids, many erotic and beautiful love poems to satisfy any passionate heart.

Almost every major and minor poet in Persia composed at some time in the *ruba'i* form.

Note: See 'Comparative Grammar, Lecture 6' in 'Lectures on the Science of Language' 1861 By Max Muller, Reprint Munshi Ram Manohar Lal, Delhi, 1965.
The Encyclopaedia Britannica Volume xxi, Eleventh Edition Cambridge 1911 (Pages 246-8).

The Ghazal.

There is really no equivalent to the *ghazal* (pronounced *guz'el*) in English poetry although Masud Farzaad,* perhaps the greatest Iranian authority on Hafiz (he spent much his lifetime finding the Variorum Edition) and his *ghazals* says, the sonnet is probably the closest. As a matter of fact, the *ghazal* is a unique form and its origin has been argued about for many centuries.

Some say that the *ghazal* originated in songs that were composed in Persia to be sung at court before Persia was converted to Islam, but not one song has survived to prove this. It is also possible that originally the *ghazals* were songs of love that were sung by minstrels in the early days of Persian history and that this form passed into poetry down the ages. I find this explanation plausible for the following reasons: firstly, the word *ghazal* means 'a conversation between lovers.' Secondly, the *ghazals* of Hafiz, Sadi and others were often put to music and became songs, which have been popular in Persia from ancient times until now.

Other scholars see the *ghazal* as coming from Arabic poetry, especially the prelude to longer poems: they say that this prelude was isolated and changed, to eventually become the *ghazal*. The Arabic root of the word *ghazal* is *gazl* which means: spinning, spun, thread, twist… the form of the *ghazal* is a spiral.

Whatever the origin, by the fourteenth century the *ghazal* had become a mature form of poetry. Among the great *ghazal* writers in Persian of the past were Rudaki, Nizami, Farid ad-Din 'Attar, Rumi and Sadi; but with the *ghazals* of Hafiz and other poets in Shiraz during his lifetime this form reached its summit.

The form of the *ghazal* at first glance seems simple, but on a deeper inspection it will be found that there is more to it than one at first sees.

It is usually between five and fifteen couplets (*beyts* or 'houses'), but sometimes more. A *beyt* is 'a line of verse split into two equal parts scanning exactly alike.' Each couplet has a fixed rhyme which appears at the end of the second line. In the first couplet which is called the *matla* meaning 'orient' or 'rising,' the rhyme appears at the end of both lines. This first couplet has the function of 'setting the stage' or stating the subject matter and feeling of the poem. The other couplets or *beyts* have other names depending on their positions. One could say that the opening couplet is the subject, the following couplets the actions: changing, viewed from different angles, progressing from one point to another, larger and deeper, until the objective of the poem is reached in the last couplet. The final couplet is known as the *maqta* or 'point of section.' This couplet or the one before it almost always contains the *takhallus* or pen-name of the poet, signifying that it was written by him and also allowing him the chance to detach himself from himself and comment on what effect the actions of the subject matter in the preceding couplets had on him. Often the poet uses a play on words when he uses his own pen-name... ('Hafiz' for example, means: a preserver, a guardian, rememberer, watchman, one who knows the *Koran* by heart. 'Jahan' means: the world).

In the *ghazal* the Persian Master Poets found the ideal instrument to express the great tension between the opposites that exist in this world. Having the strict rhyming structure of the same rhyme at the end of the second line of each couplet (after the first couplet) the mind must continually come back to the world and the poem and the rhyme. But by being allowed to use any word at the end of the first line of each couplet, one can be as spontaneous as possible and give the heart its full rein. This of course happens also in the first line of the first couplet, for whatever word or rhyme-sound that comes out in the first line sets the rhyme for the rest of the *ghazal*. So the 'feeling' created by the rhyme is one that comes spontaneously from the heart, and this spontaneity is allowed to be expanded from then on in the non-rhyming lines, and to contract in those lines that rhyme, when the mind must function as an 'orderer' of the poem. This expansion and contraction, feeling and thinking, heart and mind, combine to produce great tension and power that spirals inward and outward and creates an atmosphere that I would define as 'deep nostalgia.' This deep nostalgia is a primal moving force that flows through all life, art and song, and produces within whoever comes into contact with it when it is consciously expressed, an irresistible yearning to unite the opposites that it contains. In the *ghazal* any metre can be employed except the *ruba'i* metre.

The true meaning of Sufism, apart from the recognition of God in human form as the *Qutub* or the *Rasool* or the Christ is *tassawuf...* which means to get to the essence of everything. Adam was the first poet and it is said that he named everything and invented the first alphabet from which all others come. But Adam was not only the creator of conscious language as we know it, he was also the creator of song and the perfect form through which he created songs in praise of Eve his true Beloved, her beauty was displayed in the spiral form of the *ghazal*. So, the *ghazals* he composed and sung to her before their eventual Spiritual Union were of longing and separation and those after... of the bliss of Union. He used the same form of song about other events including the great sorrow and deep nostalgia about the loss of his favourite son Abel.

Two of Arabia's most careful and serious historians Tabari (d.923) and Masudi (d.957) state that the first poem ever composed in known history was one by Adam on the death of Abel and the form was the *ghazal*.

The lands are changed and all those who live upon them,

the face of the earth is torn and surrounded with gloom;

everything that was lovely and fragrant has now faded,

from that beautiful face has vanished the joyful bloom.

What deep regrets for my dear son... O regrets for Abel,

a victim of murder... who has been placed into the tomb!

Is it possible to rest, while that Devil that was cursed

who never fails or dies... up from behind us does loom?

"Give up these lands and all of those who live on them;

I was the one who forced you out of Paradise, your room,

where you and your wife were so secure and established,

where your heart did not know of the world's dark doom!

But you, you did escape all of my traps and my trickery,

until that great gift of life… upon which you did presume

you went and lost… and from Aden the blasts of wind,

but for God's Grace, would've swept you like a broom!"

It is said that thousands of years after Adam, the Perfect Spiritual Master Noah, settled Shiraz after his ark landed in the Turkish lands on the mountains of Ararat and was a vintner who brought the first vines that he carried with him was also a poet who composed in this form as did the *Qutub* of some three thousand years later who also settled his people he had led from their homeland in Bactria (northern Afghanistan) to Fars (Persia)… Zoroaster.

His *gathas* or hymns are in rhyme-structure the first two couplets of the *ghazal* that would later be known as the *ruba'i*.

And so the *ghazals* of the Zoroastrians were sung in their winehouses and fire temples throughout our land until the Muslim Arabs invaded and converted most to Islam, but poets and minstrels would not give up their much loved eternal God-given *ghazal* or the wine of Noah as well, which had its distant progeny in the *mesqali* grape.

The clandestine winehouses run by the Zoroastrians and Christians became the venues for many hundreds of years of the *ghazal*. In these winehouses Persians could criticise their Arab and Turkish rulers and their police chiefs and false Sufi masters and hypocritical clergy who censored and forbade them to practice the drinking of wine and the appreciation of beautiful faces and forms of unveiled women and handsome young men. In the winehouses the truth could be told and this truth was quickly spread by the minstrels in the market places and even at court through what was becoming a popular form of expression amongst the masses. And although in fact the actual drinking of wine finally became less because of the religious restrictions, it as a symbol of truth, love and freedom became more widespread.

Of course there always existed another 'Winehouse' where the Wine of Divine Love and Grace was poured out by the Winebringer or *Qutub*, the Perfect Master or the Old Magian. Here the wine and truth that flowed freely from heart to heart was of the spiritual nature and made the lover or drunkard so intoxicated with the Divine Beloved that he became *mast-like*... mad with longing to be united with the Eternal One, Whose beauty he saw and appreciated in the face and form and personality of his earthly beloved whom he praised, wooed, begged, cajoled, described, desired and desperately longed for through his *ghazals* and by his actions and with each breath of his whole life he came closer to the Eternal Beloved. Human love became transmuted into Divine Love. Although the poets of the *ghazal* may appear to many as open-minded, drunken, outcast lovers, it does not necessarily mean that they all drank the juice of the grape... for it is an inner state that they often were expressing. The *ghazal* is a conversation between the lover and the beloved and as in all intimate conversation... the talk flows both ways.

Hafeez and his Poems by Masud Farzaad. Stephen Austin & Sons Ltd. Hertford, 1949.

The Qasida

This kind of poem resembles a *ghazal* in many ways except that it is longer than the *ghazal* and is often as long as a hundred couplets. In the first couplet, both the lines rhyme, and the same rhyme runs through the whole poem, the rhyme-word being at the end of the second line of each couplet (after the first couplet) as in the *ghazal*. The *qasida* (which means 'purpose') is usually written in praise of someone and is often read in his or her presence, so it is stated that it shouldn't be too long or it might weary the listener. It has a number of sections: i. *matla* - the beginning, ii. *taghazzul* -introduction, iii. *guriz* - the couplets in praise of whoever it is written to, iv. *maqta*- the end. In the *qasida*, the *takhallus* or pen-name of the poet usually does not appear, and if it does it is not necessarily near the end or at the end as in the *ghazal*. Any metre may be used except that used for the *ruba'i* .

The Qit'a

The *qit'a* or 'fragment' must consist of at least two couplets and is similar to a *ghazal* or a *qasida* with the second lines of the couplets all having the same rhyme… but in the first couplet the double-rhyme does not usually appear. It can be composed in any metre except for that of the *ruba'i*. It can be a fragment from a *qasida* or a *ghazal,* or it may be complete in itself. Rudaki and

others often used this form to write obituaries on people whom

he knew as did many other poets.

Selected Bibliography

Divan-i Rudaki, ed. by Jahangir Mansur, Nahid, Tehran 1995.

A Thousand Years of Persian Ruba'iyat by Reza Saberi. Ibex Publishers Maryland 2000. (Pages 19-24).

Father of Persian Verse: Rudaki and his Poetry. Sassan Tabatabai, Leiden University Press, 2010.

A Literary History of Persia Vol 1 From the Earliest Times to Firdawsi By Edward G. Browne. London 1902. (pp. 455-458)

History of Iranian Literature by Jan Rypka et al. D. Reidel Publishing Company Holland. 1968 (Pages 144-5 et al.)

Golden Treasury of Persian Poetry by Hadi Hasan. Delhi 1966. (Pp 4-12).

Classical Persian Literature by A.J. Arberry. George Allen & Unwin. London. 1958. (Pages 32-37 et al.).

Borrowed Ware: Medieval Persian Epigrams, Translated by Dick Davis. Mage Publishers, 1997. (Pages 39-41.)

Early Persian Poetry by A.V. Williams Jackson: Macmillan New York. 1920. (Pages 32-45 et al.).

Music of a Distant Drum: Classical Arabic, Persian, Turkish and Hebrew Poems, Translated by Bernard Lewis. Princeton University Press. 2001 (Pages 91-99 et al.).

An Invitation to Persian Poetry, Translated from the Persian by Reza Saberi. Ketab Corp., Los Angeles, 2006. (Pages 1-4).

The Beharistan (Abode of Spring) By Jami. Translation from Persian by Edward Rehatsek. Kama Shastra Society, Benares, 1887. (Pages 133-5).

The Ilahi-nama or Book of God of Farid al-Din 'Attar Translated by John Andrew Boyle, Manchester University Press, 1976. (Page 319).

Chahar Maqala (Four Discourses of Nidhami-I-Arudi-Samarqandi, Translated by E. G. Browne, Luzac, London 1921. (See pages 49-56).

Development of the Ghazal and Khaqani's Contribution: A Study on the Development of Ghazal and a Literary Exegesis of a 12th c. Poetic Harbinger: Alireza Korangy Isfahani. Harvard University 2007. (UMI microform 3265145). (Pages 142 et al.)

The restored tomb of Rudaki in Panjkent, Tajikistan (Wikipedia).

Sculpture of Rudaki in Dishanbe, Tajikistan (Wikipedia).

Rudaki Park, Dushanbe, Tajikstan (Wikipedia).

Statue of Rudaki in Istravshn, Tajikistan (Wikipedia).

Ruba'is...

Forensic facial reconstruction of Rudaki by
Mikhail Gerasimov. (Wikipedia)

With what one has, be satisfied,

live freely:

by any formality do not be tied…

live freely!

Don't feel self-pity if others seem better off:

many more are by fortune tried.

Live, freely!

No sun blazes in this world, more than the face

of Yours!

No light graces this world, more than that grace

of Yours!

Let not one other ever be as spoiled as I am by You...

and each day may not a face seen, be even a trace

of Yours!

Your heart seems to never get tired of this cruelty,

and eyes never fill with tears when looking at me:

a hundred thousand enemies can't match You, but

still, more than my soul, I love You! I guarantee!

Heart's affair with your long hair,

stayed entangled:

much longing in these veins, here,

stayed entangled.

Only hope of relief I had was weeping: ah, no...

night of union, in my throat, there,

stayed entangled.

You, who stole the rose's perfume and colour... you

stole scent for your hair, for your face its colour too.

When washing your face stream takes on a rosy hue:

you let down hair, alley smells of musk... all through.

O one desired, for fruit in this orchard don't be

looking:

whenever you look at me, your eyes are never

watering.

Don't stay here, hopeless… the Gardener is after you:

understand it like dust that's settled and wind

blowing.

Although heart bleeds in such sorrow

of separation,

joy is more than grief: the 'tomorrow'

of separation.

I think each moment, I imagine and I wonder how

will union be... if like this is the 'now'

of separation.

Except for misfortune, I am sought...

by no one;

except a fever, warmth I am brought

by no one.

And if my soul to my lips does rise, any water

except by my eyes, is given a thought

by no one.

If you let your hair down a long night

is spread out:

if you open hair, eagle's claw in sight,

is spread out.

And if you disentangle your hair's twists and curls,

laps full of musk… a fragrant delight,

is spread out.

I hear your name... this heart of mine is delighted,

you turn your face this way, and I am overjoyed...

if someone mentions anything but you, anywhere,

my mind by a thousand sorrows becomes agitated.

When you find me deceased with lips open wide,

body with spirit gone and desires no more inside;

sit by my bier and with all your charm say this...

"O killed by me, I regret and to repent I've tried!"

For that hostile, spiteful sweetheart I went looking:

all the world with a sorrowful heart, I was roaming.

I stopped walking many times when feet hit a rock:

hand hit head so many times… it stopped thinking.

Wine is such, if a drop in the Nile falls for moment,

a sober crocodile will be drunk forever... by its scent

and, if a deer out on the plains, drinks just one drop,

it becomes a fierce lion, fear of the tiger not evident!

I am not dyeing this hair of mine

black

to be young again… to sin, to go

back;

like people dye clothes black, to mourn:

mourning my old age… I dye hair

black.

In Your name the day its banner is raising...

for You:

like Your cup, the crescent moon is waiting,

for You.

The relentlessness of Your will is copied by destiny,

and Your mercy is our daily bread, begging

for You!

At dawn that one, my beloved, came to me…

afraid of that guardian her father, obviously.

I then planted two kisses upon her moist lips:

not really lips, more like cornelian, all sugary!

It is not necessary for people to be kind, generous;

but to be thankful for grace is a must, I'm serious.

My Lord, goes on giving more than I ever need...

and so how could I not give back what is obvious?

Your letter in front of me I set down eagerly

to see...

like the Pleiades on shirt, fall tears from me

to see.

Then... as I take up my pen to reply with a letter,

I long to fold heart in it, for you eventually

to see!

Our rug in the house of grief... be spreading

we have;

crying tears, a heart that is on fire, burning,

we have.

Every tyranny this world has, been taking...

we have;

become what days of evil with are playing,

we have.

Like with Rudaki love wore me out, tired of living

I am:

my lashes are coral from bloody tears, weeping…

I am.

The agony of separation has struck fear into my soul:

like who in hell are living, from jealousy, burning

I am.

That one sold a meeting for my heart, fair

enough.

That one sells for a soul a kiss. Compare?

Enough?

When such a beauty is dealing kisses are sold

for souls, encounters for hearts anywhere!

Enough!

Rudaki, will play the harp, as he does play, drink wine:

ruby wine or liquefied ruby, none who sees it can divine

as Nature from one, made solid gem or grape for wine:

untouched it stains fingers; untasted it head makes fine.

When killing you, Fate no regrets was feeling...

for your youth and beauty no heart was having.

I find that Thief amazing... without any shame

before such a beautiful one... your life stealing.

All marble of grief from my eyes drawn by

you

pierced my cheeks that roses of secrets did

imbue.

The secrets that from my soul my heart was hiding,

my tears in language of bliss were telling,

true.

Let us drink wine, now that we're inebriated;

from hands of beauties let us get intoxicated.

The people are saying we are senseless, mad:

we are not that or that, we are drunk, stupid!

All of the flowers have come back into

the garden...

it's season once again for the meadow,

the garden.

The flames of autumn's last month have died

and now tulip's flames are on show...

the garden!

These eyes are an ocean and fire in my heart is

roaring…

between ocean and the fire how can pupil be…

surviving?

A bite of a crocodile that one has, at the heart

tearing…

that one is so cruel that if I give heart I will be

suffering!

That sneaky one, Ayar, a note was sending

to me...

"In your poems please stop keep on referring

to me;

because of you, now me this old man is abusing:

if only God would save tyranny he's doing

to me!"

Sometimes lightning is laughing, thunder's

groaning

like a mother who thirteen-year-old bride is

mourning.

On the old willow the leaves are now silken green:

on tulip dew sits like tears lovers shed when

separating.

To this life that's passing don't get too attached,

for this world is only a game... don't be deceived.

All kindness that it may do think of as made up:

when its hardships comes, your belt be tightened.

Ghazals...

Painting of Rudaki on tiled wall in Takikistan.

Bring me that wine you could call a cup of melted ruby,

or like a sword in light of sun at noon, flashing brightly.

You could say that it is rosewater distilled until pure...

its sweetness is like the balm of sleep on eyes so sleepy.

You could call the cup a cloud and wine... drops of rain:

or joy filling heart after a prayer is answered eventually.

If wine did not exist all hearts would be bleak deserts...

if we breathed our last, seeing wine revives us instantly!

And if an eagle swoops to take the wine into the sky out

from here, who would not shout... "Well done!" like me?

Of the agonies from separation much more I have suffered,

than any human being through all ages that have passed...

this heart has now forgotten all that sweet union's charms,

but, what joy after separation if one's darling has returned!

And so, I turned back happily towards the camp and tent...

spirits lightened, light-hearted and my speech enlightened;

and there came enthralled to greet me with breast heaving,

a sweet maid of cypress figure, hair to waist... that flowed.

"How has your heart been without me?" She said, flirting.

"And, how was your soul also?" She added, face going red.

Then I spoke to answer that one, "O face of heaven born...

soul's ruin, mischief-maker of all beauties upon earth's bed,

my world's snared in twist of your curls, sweet as amber...

and was hit like a ball by the polo-bat of your hair, curved!

I am full of deepest anguish from your eyes darting arrows,

I am in pain from your long locks that musk has showered!

Where is night without the moonbeam, day without a sun?

Where's rose with no water, field where it has not rained?"

Then breast became sweet, playing with her hyacinth hair,

lips from kisses from that fair coral mouth became sugared.

Now that one became the ruby-buyer and I the ruby-seller,

as she poured me wine like nectar, and the goblet I drained.

Exactly as it should be, is everything…

be happy because now joy's happening!

Why be worried… why be so sorrowful?

What is right for you, destiny is doing.

For you a minister's way doesn't work,

what is for you… fate will be deciding.

Another like you life will never make…

your mother another you isn't bearing.

Upon you God never the door closes…

before many better doors isn't opening!

Whether life is short, whether it's long,

it always ends in death... am I wrong?

No matter how long it happens to be...

through ring the cord has to pass along.

One can choose work and difficulties...

or ease where nothing ever goes wrong.

From this world one can take not much,

or... Taraz to Ray, take all there along.

It is all a dream, all that you think are...

remember that dreams do not last long.

All us are the same when death arrives,

all are identical and life cannot prolong.

If flirtation is only for beautiful ones...

then only to you does flirtation belong?

The dignity in man wine goes on revealing;

one coins buy from the free, it's separating.

Noble from base, wine tells the difference...

in the wine-cup many a talent it is holding.

When one is drinking the wine it is joyful...

even more so when the jasmine's blooming.

Many a fortress has been climbed by wine:

colts with new saddles it broke... limping.

Drinking such wine... many a tight miser

over this world generosity was spreading.

I had no chance at all to say that I am sorry

for all I did... but that One still forgave me.

It's God Whom I worship, my One creator:

my mouth praised His servants constantly.

This wheel of life's only chains and tricks...

gold-plated zinc or poison hidden in honey.

New violets have bloomed time and again:

like flames that sulfur bruised... suddenly.

When the sun is out, pour it out and drink:

passing lips in the cheeks it glows warmly.

The song of the moaning zither at sun's rising,

more than any prayer, these ears are soothing.

Is it any wonder then that the cry of the zither

the prey out of thicket into the field is luring?

The heart is always pierced by its sound even

though it is without arrows... that are flying.

It is weeping sometimes, wailing sometimes,

until dawn arrives, until night from morning.

It does not have any tongue yet it can speak:

a tale all about the lovers it's always telling.

It's able to make a mad man sane sometimes:

then, it will a sane man in chains be placing!

The wind that from Bokhara, my way

blows…

musk, roses, jasmine… breeze today

blows.

Each male or female this wind caresses, cries…

"This wind from Khutan I would say.

blows!'

From Khutan such a delicious wind won't come:

from breast of beloved without delay

blows.

I gaze towards Yemen nightly until you come…

you are star Canopus, that all away

blows.

Dearest, your name from others I try to hide…

so others mouths won't on it convey,

blows!

Yet whether I want or not, if I talk to another,

your name from my mouth in a spray

blows.

Your amber-scented hair, I wish to be stroking…

jasmine petals of your face with kisses painting.

If upon this earth you would put only one foot…

to it a thousand bows of prayers, I'd be making.

A thousand times seal upon your letter I'll kiss

if on it the mark of your signet ring I am seeing.

Tell them, "With Indian sword cut off my hand

if towards you one day, any hand I am raising!"

When I should've sung some songs I was silent;

but, to compliment you, tongue is now turning.

Musk, ambergris and a hundred-petaled rose...

white jasmine and apples and perfumed leaves.

Your beauty is containing all these and more...

Beautiful one, you capture kings, one believes.

The Night of Power*is the night of your lover,

when the veil from your face the lover relieves.

Behind a veil the sun is hiding its bright face,

when from behind your face two tulips it sees.

It's true your chin could be likened to an apple:

that apple has a mole of musk creating unease.

*Note: The night that Prophet Mohammed received the Koran's first
revelation.

My beloved's gone so I am allowed to be moaning

like at dawn how nightingale for red rose is crying.

And if you are not given to me by destiny's design

then with flames from my heart fate I'll be burning.

And, when your face you make shine so brightly…

a thousand moths and I, around you will be dying.

If, for a moment by my grave you sit and grieve…

under the tombstone I'll not remain there laying.

This world, it will be staying the same forever…

my dear, it forever and forever… will be staying.

With only one revolution, it… a king will make;

a king with a throne and a crown and an earring.

World, you made each one be rotting in the earth:

and upon them the earth more suffering is piling.

Be bringing some wine to me now that gives life,

and under the grinding stone the past be crushing.

O my dear heart why are you so self-centered,

why?

Why uselessly love the enemy? Let it be said,

why?

Why, why be seeking faith from those unfaithful…

and why be striking iron that is cold… dead,

why?

Another thing, you with your cheeks like the lily…

of your beauty lily is jealous… it, does dread,

why?

Then, reach the end of this street going nowhere…

a fire under all in it you light, none asked,

'Why?'

Your love is a mountain and my heart is a grain…

why crush a grain under a mountain bed…

why?

Ah, my dear one, forgive me, please forgive me...

to, needlessly a lover like me, make dead...

why?

Come here straight away and look at Rudaki...

if you wish to see a walking body... dead,

why?

Fragrance of stream Muliyan to me

keeps coming:

friends left behind into my memory,

keeps coming.

Sands of the Oxus bank, although they are rough,

beneath our feet as soft and silky…

keeps coming.

See greeting of the Jihan, joyful at friends return…

rising waist-high to embrace fondly,

keeps coming.

O Bokhara, live for a long time and be happy… for

joyfully your prince, your life to see,

keeps coming.

Bokhara, you are the moon and your prince the sky:

into the sky's vault, moon obviously

keeps coming.

Bokhara is the garden and the prince is a cypress...

cypress to the garden to grow freely

keeps coming. *

That perfumed hair of yours, to be holding…

I want;

on your jasmine leaves kisses to be planting,

I want.

To continue to make prostrations by the thousand

upon any path upon which you are walking

I want

to do, and for a letter a thousands kisses I'd give

if its seal had your ring's stamp, that seeing

I want.

If with a Hindu sword they cut off my hand then

I'd your lovely arm not hold, though grasping

I want!

I have to go on saying poems even if I was quiet:

tongue without end your beauty to be praising

I want.

Well done... your great beauty redefining beauty

is,

your hair's hyacinth in scent musk surpassing...

is!

And upon your icy-cold heart that than any jagged

rock a thousand times more hard, more freezing

is,

I'm now swearing that I expect no justice from you.

O you, hard of heart and cruel, who it expecting

is?

I'd be praying to the Almighty to be interceding...

but, why even bother? To God your ear turning

is?

Yet, if you chose Rudaki as a slave I'd not be one

to one who even like a thousand Darius' being

is. *

*Note: Darius the Great, the third king of the Persian Achaemenid Empire, reigned from 522 B.C. to 486 B.C.

With those with joyful black eyes live happily,

because this world is a passing illusion, only.

Be content with any surprise fate's bringing...

and all the sorrows of the past forget quickly.

Me and those fragrant curls, sweet, musky...

me and bathed in moonlight that smiling *huri!*

One who gives freely, who enjoys is fortunate,

one never doing this, never tasting joy will be!

We are brought sadness by life, a fickle wind,

so let be what comes and the full cup pass me.

I swear now to You and on my life I'm swearing

that I'll never leave You and I'll not be listening

to advice of friends who think they know better:

good advice isn't worth half our vows rejecting.

This, I have heard… that those finding heaven,

are those who 'yes' to a hopeful heart are saying.

No heart of hawk is in a thousand partridges…

no heart of God in a thousand devotees is being.

If king of Kotan even had one look at Your face,

he would fall to knees... his wealth be forfeiting.

And, if some Hindu Raja saw one hair of Yours,

he'd destroy all idols and himself be prostrating.

I'm stuck in a crossbow of torture like Abraham:

Your love will me, into regret's fire, be releasing.

Lily of paradise, be healthy and prosper always!

Prayer-arch of the faithful, is Your face, shining!

Those soft notes of the lute during the morning,

more than critical talk are much more pleasing.

Is it a wonder that its coaxing, sobbing sounds

entice wild things from where they are hiding?

That one's form is no arrow, but not only once

but each time, arrows at my heart is shooting!

And, now and then with only one tragic note,

these plaintive melodies one again is hearing

playing each day from dawn to another dawn,

due to the sound great miracles one is seeing.

Through the tongueless lovers tales are told:

sometimes the madman sane they're making,

and at times the sane by them are captivated

and bound up in chains they are them leaving.

Sweetest melody, wine... many coloured,

and like the moon, that beautiful beloved

lovely enough to an angel be captivating:

such a sight as this can I have witnessed?

To do this would make in all of my fertile

land only narcissus to be again sprouted!

None, who the beloved has stolen soul...

can now believe one's self... ever existed!

That one's so proud that one sees nothing

even when daylight is brightly displayed,

yet... that one does see each small flicker

in the eyes at night who that one adored.

When at a table of such a host so base,

best with a finger first the soup taste...

and never let the water served lips wet,

in cup is only black oil, be not in haste!

And, that kebab, never even taste it...

though delicious, poison it will encase!

Go in the world hopeless, heart broke:

its branches drips camphor, all waste!

Due to Salma's* flirtations heart feels despair:

I feel like Majnun did about Layla's long hair!*

Agony goes if you smile, but... if you turn with

a sour face, I'm healed, desire... will disappear!

At that cheerful mouth of yours the cup smiles

as your hair hypnotises, leaning upon your ear.

Babel's magic your narcissistic beauty betters:

your rose lips adds to miracles of Moses, dear.

*Notes: Salma is an ancient Arabic name for the beloved used by many Persian poets including Hafiz. Majnun & Layla are the great tragic lovers of Arabia that inspired Shakespeare to write Romeo & Juliet. The greatest masnavi poem about them is by Nizami... see my translation of this, New Humanity Books, 2006. For Majnun's own Poems see my 'Poems of Majnun' New Humanity Books, 2012.

Qasidas...

Russian statue of Rudaki

Ah me… each tooth has broken, dropped, or is near decay:

it wasn't a tooth, no… more like some lamp's brilliant ray!

All were white, flashing like silver, pearl and coral shining:

glistening like morning stars, or raindrops sparkling away.

Not one stays with me, lost through decay or being weak:

who is at fault? "Surely it's due to Saturn's rule," you say.

No, it wasn't Saturn's fault, nor the days many turnings…

"What was it?" I'll honestly say: "God's care on display!"

The world's always like this, ball of dust as it always was:

a ball of dust it'll always be, as long as this law does stay.

That thing which once healed can become a source of pain:

that thing now so painful could be a healing balm one day.

Time, at the same time, brings age, where once was youth;

and at the same time, rejuvenates what has passed away!

There exists many a desert where once was a fair garden:

a joyful garden exists, where a sad desert once held sway.

O you of moon-face, musky-hair, how could you ever know

what your poor slave once was, so esteemed, before today?

Now on me, your curling hair you so flirtatiously bestow,

in those days you did not see me, my hair grew every day.

Those darling guests of mine so full of beauty and charm…

guests who will never be returning, no matter what I say.

There were many beauties that came confusing everyone,

my eyes were always bewildered by their beauty, in array.

There was a time when I from happiness, joyfully did go,

enjoying pleasure to excess, depleting silver as I did pay.

In the market I bought, those priced above others… every

captive female Turk with pomegranate breasts that sway.

Ah… so many beautiful women, whose hearts loved me,

by night came like pilgrims to me… secretly there to stay!

And, O so many who were afraid to come in the daylight,

out of fear of their masters and fear in jail they could stay.

Sparkling wine, ravishing eyes and faces of deep beauty…

high-priced elsewhere, at my door they asked for little pay.

Because, this heart of mine was a great treasury of riches,

so full of riches that we still call love and poetry… today.

I was always happy and never knew the pain of suffering

and my heart was opened to music, like the wide highway.

Many hearts were made soft as silk by my poetry's magic,

yes… even if as hard as flintstone, or anvil heavy and grey.

My keen eyes were always open for long curls of a female:

alert ears always listening, for minstrel's latest wordplay.

I'd no house, wife, nor child… no, and no female attached;

free from all these, no responsibilities… free in every way!

Rudaki's sad situation in old age, wise one, you can verify:

in those days you didn't see me as this wretch I am today.

You didn't see me way back when rambling in this world,

singing songs, like a nightingale, a thousand tales to say.

No longer am I a friend of the nobility and the days have

long gone when it was princes who favoured in every way.

And, at the court of the king my many volumes of poetry,

were held in such high esteem, my words often held sway.

There was a time when my poems all the world repeated...

I was hailed all over as the poet of Khurasan... every day.

Who had greatness... who had favour, of all of the people?

My greatness and favour in Samanid heirs' hands did lay.

Nasr the Amir of Khurasan, gave forty thousand *dirhams,*

a fifth was added by the brave, pure prince, straight away!

From his nobles, scattered all over... sixty thousand more:

in those time when I had a fortune, a fortune in every way!

Now, the times have changed, I too, changed and must be:

bring beggar's staff to me, time for staff and writing today.

The mother of wine, should be sacrificed...

and all her babies seized, and imprisoned:

even though it is not lawful to be tearing

from mother's breast a baby being weaned.

But, such babies as these should never be

plucked and not crushed and never killed,

until drinking their mother's milk for seven

months from early spring 'til autumn's end.

Then, it'd be proper by sword and Law to

jail in a narrow cell, mother be butchered.

With shock such as this those imprisoned

babies for at least a week will be silenced.

And then... having their senses recovered,

with burning heart they'll cry... be worried.

In spasms of grief they'll roll on their face;

fits of sorrow on backs they'll have rolled:

for a burning fire produces froth and foam

but not froth and foam like a heart burned.

They'll foam with anger, like a mad camel:

froth like the devil, who has been angered.

The warder comes, then removes the foam

so as to banish the dark... make it cleared.

When the fits are over, all is settled down,

warder the dark layer of froth has removed.

 And now, the babies bright faces begin to

sparkle like the corals and the rubies... red:

some dark red like rubies of Yemen... some

pale red like rubies Badakhshan* does shed.

If you should smell them... it is like the red

rose's scent with musk, ambergris blended.

So, they are remain in the vat... until New

Year's Day and middle of April's finished:

then, at midnight, if you uncover the vat...

you'll see a miracle: disc of sun, displayed.

And as can be seen in cup made of crystal,

the bright hand of Moses and a gem... red.

Miser will be generous and the frail, brave:

one sip, pale cheeks a rose garden will bed.

And the one who a cup joyfully is drinking

will be feeling no pain or grief, in the head.

Sent to Tangiers will be grief of ten years

from Oman and Ray* new hope's arrived.

Its shirt has become worn after fifty years

because of this wine... that's so well aged.

A feast that is fit for a king will be ours...

that's with mallow, rose, jasmine adorned.

In every direction heaven sends its grace...

it makes something, impossible to copied:

new rugs and clothes with threads of gold,

flowers of far-off places, cushions spread;

the harp of 'Isa making the heart overflow,

lute of Madaknir, Chabak-e Janan fluted.*

The amirs... Bal'ami are all sitting in rows,

nobility and the elders... all, so respected.

Up at the front on the throne the king sits,

Amir of Khorasan... of all kings, the lord.

And ready to serve are a thousand Turks,

all them a two-week old moon... perfumed;

and each one's wearing a fragrant garland,

with cheeks of rosy wine and hair braided.

More fair than the fair is the winebringer,

child of a ruler and Turkish beauty, unwed.

From one to another wine's passed happily

the king of the world laughs, so contented

taking wine from angelic, dark-haired Turk

with a form like a cypress and hair tousled.

And then, the king he raises a cup of wine

and the king of Sistan is happily saluted.

He drinks, salutes... friends do the same:

each one with wine's joyfully intoxicated.

They drink to the greatest of free men and

Persia's pride... Ahmad ibn Mohammed:

the sun of his age and the lord of fairness,

through him justice is lighting the world.

If you will not accuse me of exaggeration

I'd say no one was born like him, or bred!

He is the shadow of God... God's proof:

the *Koran* says, "To him, be submitted."

From earth, water, fire, wind we're made:

king, from sun of Sasan's line, is created.

Through this one this dark land is bright,

and an Eden is this world once wretched.

Talk of grace of him, if you are eloquent:

praise him only with pen if word-crafted.

If being a philosopher you seek his way...

learn what he believes, don't be mislead.

You will say, "In wisdom... the Greeks,

Plato and Socrates are here, in his head."

If you state you're a man of God; Shaf'i,

Abu Hanifeh, Sofyan... here are seated. *

And if he speaks of the ways of wisdom,

wisdom of Luqman is in... what he said. *

One literate will get wisdom, knowledge:

wise will receive faith, be well-mannered.

And if it's an angel that you are seeking,

that Rizvan's in front of you is accepted. *

At this one's beautiful, fair face look hard

and you'll see what I say isn't overstated.

That one is kind-hearted and never false,

that one is noble, forgives when needed.

If the words of that one on your ears fall,

all ill-fortune of Saturn will be reversed.

If on his throne you see that one sitting

you'll declare, "Solomon has returned!"

Like Sam* he rides and if the stars stay

no horse will see a one so accomplished.

When battle comes with hate, bravery...

and when he in helmet, armour, is spied,

even the elephant will be seen as small...

even an elephant roaring... intoxicated.

When in midst of battle, even Isfandiyar*

would run from his spear, as he trembled!

His mountain of a body in peaceful times

is Mount Siyam,* none see him flustered.

And even a dragon will melt like wax if he

faces that one's spear, it's as if fire's faced.

And, if Mars should arrive in the battle...

by his sword Mars will be eaten... gutted.

When again he takes in his hand the wine,

no spring cloud like him... has ever poured.

It is only dark rain spring clouds shower...

bags of gold and rolls of silk he has rained.

With his hands he goes on giving, giving:

he rains so much a storm seems wasted.

One could say it is the grace of that one

giving real value... to when he is praised.

The poor poet with his empty hands goes

to him, and with much gold is showered.

With much praise he's caressing the poet:

one is hired at court if one is one learned.

When it comes to justice and fairness...

none is as honest or fair when compared.

From him weak and strong receive justice:

no hatred or tyranny by him is displayed.

All over the world his grace is abounding,

and... no one of his grace is ever deprived.

He comforts whom the world is troubling

and the heart-broken he has always helped.

This glorious king's merciful, true nature...

bound all deserts and fields, them lassoed.

He pardons sins and remorse is accepting,

he doesn't get angry, by forgiveness is led.

This one is Sistan's lord, victorious king...

with luck of tiger, enemy a deer entrapped.

In that one is seen rebirth of Amr Lays, *

with his entourage and times reproduced.

The name of Rustom's great, but the son

of Dastan because of him is remembered.*

O Rudaki, stop your praising of another,

praise only him, wealth's seal's received.

It does not matter the effort you put in...

or if you use a file to make wit sharpened,

to compose poems worthy is impossible...

but bring what one has, however unsuited.

And so, here is a eulogy, as good as I can:

there are fine words in it, it is easily said.

Words right for the Amir I don't have but

my poems Jarir's, Tai's, Hassan's rivaled.*

Praise to the Amir, the world praise him:

from him beauty, order, virtue are spread.

Ah no... my poems show how weak I am:

although like Sahban and Sari I'm gifted.*

At the present time this eulogy I present,

I who at praising kings is I say, perfected.

To praise all of mankind has its limitation:

to praise him there is no way to be limited.

No wonder Rudaki can't rise to this event:

without speech or soul he is now stupefied.

If Bu 'Omar hadn't encouraged me again,

if the minister, Adnan, me hadn't allowed,*

how would I've been brave enough to praise

the Amir for whom God the world created?*

And if I was not helpless and weak, and if I

from the Amir of the east was not ordered,

I would've been running like some servant

with poem in my teeth, to him to be heard.

This poem is my apology, from me to you...

as a knower of words you will have realized

that the excuse of your servant is old age...

that is why as your guest I haven't arrived.

May always be soaring glory of my Amir,

so that his foes always failing, will be dead.

As high as the moon his head be reaching...

and under the fish all his enemies be buried.

More brilliant than the sun may his face be,

than Judy, Sahlan, his grace be prolonged. *

All of you, who are sad, all you who are suffering,

all who hide your tears that from eyes are flowing

for that one... whose name I do not now mention,

because more sorrow and difficulty I am fearing...

what has gone has gone and what came... is here,

what was... was, so, why uselessly be mourning?

To this world you desire to give peace, friendship?

World from you, peace, friendship isn't accepting!

Don't be complaining, it isn't hearing complaints:

and, as it does not hear you... stop all your crying!

Even if you go on crying until Day of Reckoning,

can one who left be brought back by your crying?

From this wheel of life you will see more torture,

if at each of its turns you take on more suffering.

It is like as though, tragedies have been given to

the one to who your heart you have been giving.

No clouds have appeared and no eclipse arrived:

yet, moon is not visible and the earth darkening.

I don't like saying but whether or not you agree,

you will never be able to yourself be conquering.

To be breaking the siege of grief upon your heart

the best thing to do is this… wine, be drinking!

Eventually from any great disaster such as this,

goodness and grace and nobleness… is coming. *

*Note: It is said that this poem was composed upon the death of the father of Rudaki's patron Amir Ahmad ibn Isma'il, Amir Isma'il-ibn Ahmad… who passed on in 907 A.D. It could of course be about another as no one is mentioned by name.

A verdant spring is here, full of colour and bright,

many thousands of decorations, things to delight.

It is only right that old men become young again

in a world that changes old for young, overnight.

A great army has been put on display by the sky:

led by a breeze... an army of clouds dark as night.

Its drum is its thunder; its lighting, swords flash!

A thousand armies I saw, none so ready to smite.

See how that cloud is weeping like a man in grief:

like a distressed lover, thunder moans its plight.

Out from the clouds the sun occasionally looks,

like a prisoner hiding from guard with foresight.

This world that for a while has suffered... finds

cure from jasmine-scented breeze, for its plight.

In waves showers of musk are streaming down,

on the leaves a new silken sheen, shining bright.

Roses now bloom from cracks, instead of snow:

streams once dry, flow quickly, at some height.

Thunder's moaning like wind over the meadow,

while from clouds lighting cracks whip, a sight!

In the distance upon the meadow a tulip smiles,

like a bride's nails painted with *henna* to excite.

Out from the willow the nightingale is singing:

starling is answering, from the cypress' height.

From the cypress the dove's old tune is echoing

as nightingale woos the red rose, as is its right.

Now is the time to drink the wine... be happy:

now is the time for the lovers and their delight.

Pick out your winebringer and wine, and drink!

Sing like nightingale or starling, nothing trite!

Although it is a sight to see, this new spring...

compared to joy in seeing my lord it's no sight.

During your old age like when you were young,

all of us have marveled at you... day and night.

You brought into being many dreams you had:

from you comes majesty, joy, all things bright.

May our glorious ruler a long time be living;

and my valuable life to that one's be adding.

About that one's life, I am always worried...

unique since free bears mother was birthing.

A youth like this monarch has never existed:

literate and full of wisdom, brave, forgiving!

How hard that one tries, can another know:

how generous that one is... one, is knowing?

That one with tongue, hand, scatters pearls:

through this world that one's name is going!

In hearts that one planted seed of kindness:

turning back on wealth that one isn't joking!

To tell of such grace and will is a difficulty:

in wisdom... *Avesta, Zend* in depth, rising. *

The poets all try hard but it does not work...

they way they should praise each is lacking.

Seed is that one's essence, water... is grace:

that one's fertile soil, is poet's appreciating.

That one's essence is *Vahi-nama* to Kisra:

that one's ways... is *Pand-nama* guiding.*

The true *Pand-nama* is this ruler's essence,

from such wisdom fortune can be learning.

One who turns back on advice of this ruler

into sorrow's trap the foot of joy is placing.

In this old world who's defeat's raw dough?

One who at that one's fortune isn't smiling.

To any not wishing that one a splendid life

tell this: 'Try to fortune's hands be tying!"

Angels, of that one's friends glory be proud:

heavens, at ruler's foes misery, be laughing!

With what I first said I will end this poem:

may our glorious ruler a long time be living!

*Notes: The Avesta is the sacred book of the Zoroastrians and Zend is
the interpretation of it. The Vashi-nama is a 'Book of Revelation'.
Kisra is the title of Khusrow Anushirvan (531-579) the 21st Sasanian king…
the Pand-nama or 'Book of Guidance' is attributed to him.

Qit'as...

A 'modern' bust of Rudaki

Free my soul from torment and pain

with kisses... two, or perhaps three:

and such gracious favour's reward...

the great blessing from God will be!

If to the grave I take your friendship with me,

as I praise you... to me you remain virtuous.

What the Amir left, I do not want to stay...

I want the Amir to stay here... is it obvious?

That one who left we must know he's gone:

one dead one must see as dead... oblivious!

Moon-like beauties, songs, wine rosy of hue,

would make even angels fall into a pit, too.

My gaze can't be sewn up, for on my grave

narcissi grow, weeds won't break through.

One who knows the intoxication of love...

sobriety for a time, is not right thing to do.

Eyes that by day can't see a roof's beam...

at night a straw in her eye is easy to view.

Your hair into a 'j', who… was curling?

Your mole, dot on that 'j', One created!

Plus, your mouth is so tiny it's like He

took a pomegranate seed and it halved!

My lord, the feast of Mihregan[*]

arrives...

feast of nobles and royalty, again

arrives.

Time is here to put away silk, put on fur:

tent (not into meadow or garden)

arrives.

The lily has now given way to the myrtle:

judas-tree isn't seen but red wine

arrives.

Your reign's only begun and you are kind:

luckily in your youth, mature wine

arrives.

[*]Note: An old Persian celebration of autumn.

It was close to Sarakhs that I saw a hoopoe...

whose small song to the clouds was reaching.

That one was wearing a little coat I observed

that was made up of such different colouring.

O you old world, so ugly, and so mixed-up...

before you staggered and awed, I'm standing.

The grassy meadow, winter's breath dyes

like the tails of wolves... and tigers,

too;

now like the Arzhang* is made, coloured

in this springtime of Mani's fingers,

too.

On ship of life do not get too comfortable

because the Nile has many crocodiles

too.

*Note: The Arzhang was the illustrated book of scriptures of the famous
painter and founder of Manichaeism, Mani (216-276 A.D.)

In this house, I was always intoxicated…

I was safe like the Amir and the nobility.

House, town, like me the same, rooted…

so why has joy turned to grief, suddenly?

Now, snow is covering the black mountain,

and bent like a bow in garden is the

cypress.

That, which tasted so fine is not tasty now:

that what didn't harm, now causes

distress.

Ah world, you treat your children like this...

sometimes as a mother, then a stepmother?

No need for you to have columns, braces...

no need for iron doors or stone walls either.

Totally like some dream this world is acting;

one with an open heart, this will be realizing:

cruelty here, it with kindness, is replacing...

sorrow here, it... with happiness is replacing.

With a world like this why be so contented,

for it is not right, all that is here happening.

World's face may be fine, its ways are not...

it has bad manners, although it is charming.

O friend, will you ever stop saying, "Where's joy?"

Nobody ever stops himself from eating soft *halva*.

At the moment I find it is well worth repenting…

like, when a sick person sneezes, it is a protector!

Anyone who saw that cornelian wine,

could not tell it from melted cornelian.

Both are of the same essence… but, in

nature one is solid, the other in motion.

That one as a powder colours the hand;

the other tasted, in head causes elation.

My dear boy, in this world we are only prey,

we're all just sparrows and death is a hawk.

Each rose will be dying, today or tomorrow:

under a grinding stone, death stops all talk.

All the great men of this world have passed

on...

to death, each his head bowed, and traveled

on.

All of those who great palaces were building,

now are covered with the dirt that we tread

on.

Out of many thousands of comforts they had

did any remain for them but a shroud to bed

on?

They were enjoying what they were wearing;

what they gave away... and what they fed

on.

It has no ear but speaks, it's crippled but walks,

sees the world without eyes, dumb but eloquent.

It is moving like a snake, like a sword it's sharp;

it has a dark face, like a lover body bent, spent.[*]

[*]Note: This is a riddle poem, so popular in Persia at the time of
Rudaki, and later. It is a pen. See 'Courtly Riddles. Enigmatic
Embellishments in Early Persian Poetry by A.A. Seyed-Gohrab, Leiden
University Press.

If heart's facing Bokhara and Taraz's beauties

what then's the point in God's house facing? *

Your faith in love, will be accepted by God...

but, your prayers God will not be accepting!

*Note: House of God is the Kaaba at Mecca.

If I'm not unfortunate, why am I now

with this bad-tempered, loose female?

I am thrown to the lions, she's happy:

but if a fly lands on her I'm sick, pale!

She tortures me but the love I have for

her stays in my heart: that is my tale!

No wonder roses on that one's cheeks are blooming,

for when that one takes wine... roses always

bloom.

When that one stands up in curls that hair's falling:

that one's body's in good health but eyes spell

doom.

Muradi* is dead, but it seems he has not died:

death of such a Master can be no small thing!

He has given back his dear soul to the Father,

his dark body to Mother he was relinquishing.

What belonged to the angels they now have...

the one said to be dead, has now begun living.

This one wasn't like hay the wind blew away,

this one wasn't water, cold could be freezing.

This one was no comb that hair could break...

and no seed that the earth could be crushing.

In this world that one was a golden treasure:

both worlds as a barley-grain he was seeing.

That one's shell of clay earth received again,

to heavens his soul and wisdom were rising.

His other life that most did not know about,

for God he went on polishing and entrusting.

He was the pure wine, with some sediment...

while he rose to the top then it... was settling.

My dear, all of them make the same journey...

from Marv, Ray, Rum, Kurdistan... all going!

All, are going back to their home at the end...

how can rough cloth, satin... ever be equaling?

Like a full-stop be stopping. As the Almighty

from the book of speech your name is striking!

Note: Abul Hasan Muhammad ibn Muhammad Muradi was a fellow-poet and friend of Rudaki, but not many of his poems have survived.

The caravan of Shahid*has traveled on before us:

believe me when I say, ours will go on… as well.

The eye counts that there is another body fewer,

but the loss as thousands… the mind would tell.

Take as a gain everything enriching your soul…

before death arrives, ties your legs then farewell!

Everything that you've tried so hard to discover,

it's best that you don't easily lose it… pell-mell.

Friend will become a stranger because of profits:

if you pay that one less… it will that spell quell.

There is no wolf that is alive as fierce as a lion…

cry of the sparrow the hawk can't hear, as well.

*Note: On the death of Shahid Balkhi (d.940) the poet and friend of
Rudaki who was also under the patronage of Amir Nasr ibn Ahmad.
He was said to be 'of excellent mind, a spirited conversationalist, with
high opinions and a scholar'. The melancholy that is in some of his poems
meant that he was eventually called, 'the pessimist of the century'.
He was said to be one of the great philosophers of his time.
For a selection of his poems see my 'Piercing Pearls: The Complete
Anthology of Persian Poetry ' Vol. One New Humanity Books 2012.

Live happily, O so happily with those dark-eyed ones,

for this world is nothing but a story of wind… passed.

One should never weep for what has happened already

and one should never be sorrowful for what has passed.

I'm happy with the musky hair of that one, ambergris

scented: with moon-like face… *huri*-like face, natured.

He happy and kind and free with himself and others…

and miserable becomes that one who to both isn't good!

It is so sad, because this world is only wind and cloud…

bring wine, for: "Whatever happens… happens," I said.

This world, it has every aspect of a dream…

that one with an awakened heart, knows this.

The good that it has replaces the bad it has…

joy that it has replaces the pain… with bliss!

How is it possible for you… to sit so easily in

this world, whose operations are often amiss?

The world may look good, but it acts so bad:

it has a pretty face but acting ugly so often is.

The world, it gave to me plenty of advice:

it's full of advice if you look at it closely...

it says, "Don't be envious of another's joy,

there are many who wish like you they be!"

By killing so many, enemy's bravery you crushed:

because of your generosity no beggar now we see!

On the tables of many are sweet dishes and lamb,

yet some are without bread and so they go hungry.

It's not right to sit always doing nothing, get up!

Your gold might reach the moon... get up quickly!

Life's like a horse, O rider, your choice to be galloping

is...

life's like a ball O polo-stick, your choice to be playing

is.

Even though the player of the harp has soft, nimble hands;

they to the hands holding pen... that one sacrificing

is.

Because of you... oppression is far less and jealousy also,

because of you much more justice and more giving...

is.

Except for love, there is no real intoxication…

even for one like you, love is enough suffering.

If in heart of your foe, thoughts of war rage…

fearing your scimitar his limbs off are falling.

Hawk and finch share sky due to your justice,

night and day embrace, as it… you're willing.

Be happy from this moment as death's wind

the trees of spiteful lies… will be uprooting.

As long as there stays a trace of this world,

while this universe's wheels go on turning…

may all wishing you well feast in happiness,

all of your glory envious from grief be crying!

Printed in Dunstable, United Kingdom